Discussion Guide Based On

# The Art of the Hustle
## Lessons In Becoming A Man

Fifteen Gentlemen share the lessons of their

childhood and early adulthood

## by

## Jo Evans Lynn &
## The Council of Elders

Discussion Guide Developed by Dr. Jo Evans Lynn

This1 Matters Foundation, Greensboro, NC 27405

Second Edition Published by:

 This 1 Matters Foundation, Greensboro, NC 27406

ISBN: 978-1-7369837-6-8

Invitation to Use The Book _The Art of the Hustle: Lesson In Becoming A Man_ To Change Lives:

You are invited to help your youth group join other young men, their fathers, and mentors in an exploration of ourselves, our families, our communities, our goals, and the world around us.

This book _The Art of the Hustle: Lesson In Becoming A Man_ by the Council of Elders and Jo Evans Lynn if read and studied as a guided reading activity has the potential to change the lives of youth everywhere. The selection of this book should be based on your recognition of the enormous challenges these gentlemen overcame to become mentors and leaders in their communities and the wonderful bonds they developed through their years of mentoring.

In order to reach his goals, every man must overcome some of the same issues that these men had to deal with in their youth. _The Art of the Hustle: Lessons In Becoming A Man_ should be an inspiration to every boy or man no matter his age. In addition, the book is a powerful tool in reinforcing our constant message that, "If you can dream it, and are willing to work for it you can achieve it."

Please encourage your mentees to invite their friends and family members to read along with them. Mentors who want to plan an event with Council of Elders, may contact us online at: https://councilofeldersinc.com/

Sincerely,

David Moore, President The Council of Elders

# Contents

PAGE

Calendar of Events................................................................. 5

Discussion Calendar ............................................................. 6

Introduction…..................................................................... 7

About the Authors................................................................ 7-9

Praise…............................................................................. 9

Pre-Reading Discussion (Themes)....................................... 10-13

Journal Writing ................................................................. 14-24

Discussion Questions ........................................................ 25-58

Summary/Enrichment Activity ........................................... 61

The  Art of the Hustle Vocabulary ...................................... 62

Paideia Seminar: The Art of the Hustle ............................... 63-64


Appendix
   Common Debate Rules for Classrooms............................. 66-67
   Personal Seminar Rating Chart ...................................... 68

# Calendar of Events

**Kick Off! Three of the Members of the Council of Elders serve as** Guest Speakers

**Art of the Hustle to Work or College, 5-mile Walk/Run** proceeds used to help sponsor a Job/Career/College Fair and College Tour.

**Sessions** for reading and discussion of the book, <u>The Art of the Hustle</u> should be spread over a 3–6-week period. *We suggest the groups are small with no more than 12 members including the mentor or group leader.*

**"Black Men Prepare for Work & College Night (Fall)**, Historically Black Colleges, Associate Degree Programs, post high school advance training programs (Police, firemen, etc.), and other work prep entities will be on hand to explain their incentive programs to increase the numbers of underrepresented groups in their professions.

**A Lunch for Hustlers (**Picnic Lunch with Paideia Sessions with Bag Lunches) at Barber Park.

**Essay Contest:** One of the reasons why this book was chosen was because the lives of themain characters "mirror" the lives of many of the young men who live in predominately black Communities throughout America. Think about the main characters and the themes of the novel. Write a 1–2-page essay titled "Empowering Black Men to Excel" discussing the role that male mentors, coaches, relatives, and teachers have played in your life, in the life of a close friend, or relative.

**"Men Mentoring the Next Generation" Dinner**, All participants and their mentors, father figures, coaches, etc., are invited for a weekend gathering. Each family will be asked to bring food that their family usually eats during their gatherings. For example, in the book John Wynn talks about the food produced by all the good cooks in his family, like succulent meat loaf, and amazing pound cake.

**Men Work! Career Fair and College Night (Spring).** Careers like firemen, law enforcement, daycare, culinary arts , auto mechanics, etc. that need two years beyond highschool or less will be featured with Historically Black Colleges and Associate Degree pro-grams.

*Synopsis: THE ART OF THE HUSTLE: LESSONS IN BECOMING A MAN  is a compilation of life lessons as told to Jo Evans Lynn by 15 members of the Council of Elders. The Council of Elders is comprised of men who have dedicated their lives to mentoring youngmen from boyhood to manhood.*

*Please read the pages noted below before each session so that you will be ready to engage in ascholarly discussion of the book.*

# Discussion Calendar

| *Sessions* | *Pages (Presession Reading)* |
|---|---|
| Day 1 | Introduction: Themes & Vocabulary |
| Day 2 | The Hustling Begins at An Early Age , p.p. 1-12 |
| Day 3 | The Village: Lessons In Community p.p. 15-27 |
| Day 4 | It's About Family p.p. 28-38 |
| Day 5 | Unconditional Love, p.p. 39-45 |
| Day 6 | When I was Nothing But A Boy, p.p. 46-52 |
| Day 7 | What About Race, 54-69 |
| Day 8 | My Brother's Keeper, p.p. 70-78 |
| Day 9 | The Keys to Living Well,  p.p. 79– 85 |
| Day 10 | The King and Queen of the House, p.p. 86– 92 |
| Day 11 | Time Management, p.p. 93-99 |
| Day 12 | Lessons Well Learned, p.p. 100-104 |
| Day 13 | Be Ready, Be Ready p.p.105-112 |
| Day 14 | Mighty Men Move Others to Greatness, p.p. 113-120 |
| Day 15 | Family, God, and Country, p.p.121-128 |
| Day 16 | Creating Leaders, p.p. 129-144 |
| Day 17 | I Still Laugh When I Think About It   145-148 |
| Day 18 | Leaving a Legacy, 149-155 |
| Day 19 | Post Reading Discussion |

*Other Events as planned. Please note that the Events and Discussion Calendar aresuggestions. Mentors may tailor events and calendars to suit the needs of your group.*

**Discussion Guide Based On**
# The Art of the Hustle:
## L e s s o n s   I n   B e c o m i n g   A   M a n

*Fifteen gentlemen share lessons about growing up as a Blackyouth in America*

## INTRODUCTION

They grew up in communities in North Carolina, Wisconsin, South Carolina, and Washington, D.C. Their stories teach very vivid lessons about growing from boyhood to manhood in predominately Black communities during the forties, sixties, seventies, and eighties. However, the lessonsof Black manhood-working to provide for one's family, and being emotionally connected to one's sons, are timeless.

This is a book about the power of family, community, education, and faith. These are stories of joining forces and beating the odds. It is a book about changing your life, and the lives of others ...together.

## ABOUT THE AUTHORS

**Thomas Alan Bell** was born and raised in Philadelphia, Pennsylvania. He graduated from North Carolina State University with a degree in Industrial Education. After graduating, he settled in Greensboro, North Carolina; married and raised his three children (two boys and one girl) in his adopted city. He is a member of Bethel AME Church. He has served as a mentor at several Elementary schools in the Guilford County School System.

**Ezekiel Ben-Israel-A.K.A. Robert Benson Duren, II** attended the Greensboro City Schools graduating from James B. Dudley High School in 1972. He served in the United States Air Forceas a Conscientious Objector. Although he refused to carry a gun, he served honorably as an orderlyat military hospitals in Texas and in Turkey. He has a B.A. in Industrial Technology, Manufacturing from North Carolina A&T State University and a M.S. in Counseling Psychology, Oral Roberts University. He is a Certified Counselor. He is a member and Associate Pastor at Trinity AME Zion Church.

**Timothy E. "Gene" Blackmon,** The youngest member of the *Council of Elders* is a licensed master barber with 20 years' experience. He is father of one son. He graduated from Page High School where he was a pitcher on the varsity baseball team. He is the founder of Prestige Barber College in Greensboro and a co-founder of Young Men of Promise, male mentoring program.

**Larry C. Burnett,** a native of Dunn, North Carolina, and a graduate of North Carolina A&T State University. After graduation, he joined the United States Army as a Commissioned Officer. He served 25 years in the military. Throughout his career in the military, he volunteered to mentor and coach youngsters. He is the Executive Director of Hayes-Taylor Memorial YMCA in Greensboro, North Carolina.

**McArthur Davis,** a native of Winston Salem, North Carolina is the Executive Director of the S.A.V.E.D. Foundation which is a group of Behavioral Health & Social Service Providers. He is a certified Counselor and the father of two sons and one daughter. He has mentored with MenTors and the *Council of Elders*.

**Milton "Choo Choo" Grady** was born in Washington, D.C. at the Army Hospital. He was raised by his grandparents. He has a Bachelor of Science Degree from North Carolina A&T State University. The father of one son, he has been married for 45 years. For many years he has served as a community and youth advocate. Most of his job experience has been with nonprofits. He has mentored with BOTSO, MenTors, and the *Council of Elders.*

**Arthur Johnson, Jr.,** a native of Charleston South Carolina retired from the United States Army after 22 years of service. He is also retired from the U.S. Post Office. Johnson is a member and Steward at Bethel AME Church in Greensboro. He has served as a mentor in the *Council of Elders.*

**Lt. Col. Clifton Girard Johnson (Retired)** graduated from James Benson Dudley High School in 1969. He graduated from A&T State University in 1974 with a B.S in Engineering. He also hasa master's degree from Troy State. He served 25 years in the United States Air Force.

**Rev. Alphonso McGlen,** a native of Washington D.C. entered the ministry when he was 15and was pastoring his first church at the age of 23. He entered the United States Army as an enlist- ed man and later attended Howard University and the Seminary at Shaw University. As the pastor of Bethel AME Church in Greensboro, he became involved with the mentoring programs sponsored by several of his members.

**Ralph D. Mitchell,** a native of Madison, Wisconsin is a motivational speaker. He has degrees from Knoxville College and the University of North Carolina Chapel Hill. He served in the Infantry of the United States Army where he reached the rank of First Lieutenant. He worked for many years at the Center for Creative Leadership. Mitchell is the chairman of Nehemiah-The Leadership Company. He is a member of Mont Zion Baptist Church. He has been married 45 years and has two sons and five grandchildren.

**David "Bunny" Moore,** James B. Dudley Class of 1962, Member of the Dudley High School Drum Line, and the A&T State University Drum Line. Moore is a long-time community activist, 2015 Inductee into the Dudley Hall of Distinction, Winner 2015 Alumni Service Award, volunteer, and mentor for students throughout the Guilford County School System. Moore is one of the founding members of BOTSO, MenTors, and the *Council of Elders.* In each of the groups he has served as leader or president. David Moore has been married for 53 years and is the father of one daughter and two sons.

**Robert "Bob" Purvis** is a native of Williamson, North Carolina and he graduated from E.J. Hayes High School. He has been married 51 years and is the father of three children (Two boys and one girl). He retired from Boy Scouts of America after 17 years of service. He is a founding member of Faith Community Church in Greensboro.

**James Aquilla Smith,** one of the first African American SCCA Crew Chiefs has served as a mentor with MenTors, and the Council of Elders. He founded a program for youth in 1988, Youth for Truth, which focused on reading and career prep. He also volunteers with the James B. DudleyHigh School Electric Car Team.

**Henry "Hank" Wall,** a native of High Point, North Carolina was a member of the last class to graduate from William Penn High School. He joined David Moore as one of the founding members of Bothers Organized to Save Others (BOTSO) and later mentored with MenTors and the *Council of Elders*. He served in the United States Army. Wall retired after 30 years of service from the United States Post Office. He continues to work with BOTSO; working with two chapters of the program in Greensboro and High Point, North Carolina.

**John E. Wynn** is a native of Greensboro who grew up in the Warnersville Community that was settled by former slaves and freedmen. He grew up a member of the African Methodist Episcopal Zi- on Church since early childhood. He served several tours of duty in the United States Army that took him to various places all over Europe. He says that he always made it a point to learn the language of the countries where he was deployed. After leaving the military, he worked for the government for 19 years. John has served as a mentor in BOTSO, MenTors, and with the *Council of Elders*. He was an active parent at Ben L. Smith High School, volunteering for over 10 years serving as president and vice-president of the PTA and the Athletic Boosters. He is the father of two sons and has been married for 35 years.

**Dr. Jo Evans Lynn,** a native of Greensboro, N.C. taught nearly every grade level and every form of English/language arts during her 37 years as an educator. She graduated from James Benson Dudley High School in 1967, from Shaw University in 1970 with a B.A. in English, North Carolina A&T State University in 1982 with a master's degree in Reading Education and Walden University in 2013 with a doctorate in Educational Leadership.

## Praise

"If more preachers would approach sinners like the pastor in *Beyond My Brother's Keeper* churcheswould be full to overflowing." **Mary L. Anderson**

"After you've read it, pass it on...*The Art of the Hustle: Lessons in Becoming a Man* is a book that should never end up on a shelf because it is probably the most important book for African American families that has been written since the protest era...Besides their personal stories, the men share practical steps that can be useful to a circle of boys or young men in making their own commitment to being successful in life and mentoring others… This book just may change a boy or young man's future." ⸺ **Dr. Jo Evans Lynn**

"They are an inspiration to young people everywhere, and their messages are ones that can transformthe world."⸺ **Gloria D. Evans**

# Pre-Reading Discussion

*A theme is the central idea or ideas explored by a literary work. A work of literature may have more than one theme. Before we begin reading the book* The Art of the Hustle: Lessons In Becoming A Man *by the Council of Elders and Jo Evans Lynn let us discuss some of the themes in relationship to your personal experiences, the experiences of friends or relatives or past reading.*

**Family** is perhaps the most important theme of the book. The book examines family from all sides- the positive and the negative. Each of the men talks about his family, church, and his "village" (neighborhood). Based on your experiences with your family and neighborhood, which group do you predict will have the strongest impact on the behavior of the men in elementary school? In high school? After school?

**Mainstay** is something or someone you can depend on to be there for you. Who or what are the mainstays in your life?

**The Village** community is a tribal or communal concept that is part of our African roots. It is an innate system that socially, emotionally, culturally, and economically ties together an extended family in a supportive atmosphere that includes every man, woman, and child living within a neighborhood.

**Abandonment** several of the men are abandoned to a certain degree by one or both parents. Based on your personal experiences, reading, or the experiences of others, what effect might abandonment have on a child? On a family? Is it possible to have both parents living at home and still "feel" abandoned?

**Mentorship** is another major theme of the book. A mentor is an adult who serves as a role model and advisor. Who has served as your mentor? Are your role models more likely to be celebrities or people in your immediate surroundings?

**Poverty,** especially the impact poverty has on living conditions, schools, crime, and opportunity, is an implied theme of the book. Is being poor the same as living in poverty? Explain.

**Extended Family** whether stable or unstable plays an important role in each of the lives of the authors. If you had to describe your family as a lifeboat, a Band-Aid, or wound which term would you use? Explain.

**Choices and Consequences** often people feel that everything is out of their hands- that they have no say so in what happens in their lives. However, *The Art of the Hustle: Lessons IN Becoming A Man* makes it clear that the men made choices that made a difference in their lives. Think about some major choices that you have made thus far in your life. What were some consequences that you had to face as a result of your choices? Was the effect of your choices limited to your past or are you still affected by those choices?

**Discipline**, both self-discipline and parental discipline, is also a major theme. Which type of discipline do you think is most important for young people your age? Explain.

**The ability to dream big** is another theme of the book. Some call it confidence; others refer to it as hope. Eitherway, it is manifested in one's ability to dream "big" beyond their present circumstances. What do you think happensto people who cannot dream beyond their current conditions? Why do people lose the ability to dream?

**Perseverance** is not only "hanging" in there through the bad times but fighting the good fight in the face of certain defeat. Often it is a matter of honor and ultimately one of the truest demonstrations of integrity. Can you think of someone you know who has demonstrated perseverance during difficult times?

Read the poem "A Dream Deferred" by Langston Hughes. The word *deferred* means, "to postpone or to put off until a later time." Answer the underlined question as it relates to your life or to the lives of people you know. What happens when we put our dreams off to a later time or when the dreams of those around us never seem to come true?

# A Dream Deferred
## *by Langston Hughes*

<u>What happens to a dream deferred?</u>
Does it dry up
like a raisin in the
sun?Or fester like a
sore-- And then
run?
Does it stink like rotten meat?
Or crust and sugar
over--like a syrupy
sweet?
Maybe it just
sags    like    a
heavy load. Or
does            it
explode?

**Directions:** Discuss the poem with your group. After the  discussion  you should be able to answer the following questions.

1.  What are *rhetorical questions?*

_____

_____

2.  What poetic concept is used in the first stanza?

_____

3.  Is the second stanza a question? If it is not a question, what is it?

_____

4.  What poetic concept is used in the last stanza?

_____

5. What other two poetic concepts are used in the poem?

_____

_____

## KEY THEME:

The importance of father figures is an underlying theme of the book. Is having father figures more important for boys than for girls? Explain.

_____

_____

_____

_____

# Journal Writing

During my more than thirty-seven years as a teacher, I found that journal writing is one of the most effective ways to free inhibitions about sharing personal information.  My rules are simple:

1.  Be honest with yourself. Your writing will not be checked for spelling punctuation or grammar. Just write.
2.  If you do not want to share a piece, fold the page under and sign the back of it. I will trust you to have actually written something and you can trust me not to violate your trust by reading what you have written. You may only do this twice. You must substitute that piece with another journal topic of your choice by the final turn in date.
3.  If someone chooses to share a piece, listen, and do not share his or her story with people outside this group.
4.  Don't judge and don't give unasked for advice.

Depending on the age and level of independence of the group, the mentor/teacher may select a topic for the group to write about before the session.

## Note to Readers:

Talk to your friends, siblings, or teammates  about an event or period in your life that you shared that not only had an impact on who you are now but may also impact your future. For example,  some young men might write about how each of them came to be involved in the group that is reading this book or about how the events in Middle School or  their freshman year in high school helped to mold them into the individual they are today.

**Activity Directions:** *Keep a journal of **at least six entries** about people (friends, family, teachers, mentors) and events that have had an impact on your life. Other than deciding what you will write about as a group, do not read one another's journals until each of you has written about the same topic.*

## Suggestions:

1. We are best friends because… (Write about when and how you became friends. How do you help oneanother? What are your strengths or weaknesses as friends?

2. This one time… (Write about a time that you got into BIG trouble together. What were the consequences? What did you learn from this experience?)

3. We will always be friends because…. (What will hold you together as friends after high school?)

4. Just as the group *Brothers Organized to Serve Others* has given many young men dreams for a

better future,_____gave me my dream…

5. This is my "big" dream" and here is how I will make it happen…

6. I grew up the day that… Write a 1–2-page epiphany story detailing the single event that, for you,marked your transition from childhood to adulthood.

7. This is my definition of a "real father"….

8. My___(Title: Teacher, Coach, Father, Uncle, Neighborhood, Pastor,etc.) was a "Real Father to me because…

9. Male children should no longer be called  boys when they reach the age of____ because…

10. How much responsibility should older sibling have for their younger siblings?

11. Who is your role model? How has he/she earned that role in your life?

12. What makes you special? What makes you stand out in a crowd?

13. Based on what I know from my personal experiences or from the experiences of friends or relatives who have been in foster care, these are the **first five questions** I would ask a person who wanted to become a foster parent. Here's why I feel the answers to these questions are so important.

Additional Topics:

_____

_____

_____

_____

_____

_____

_____

# Journal 1:

_____

_____

_____

_____

_____

_____

_____

_____

_____

_____

_____

_____

_____

_____

_____

_____

_____

_____

**Journal 2:**

_____

_____

_____

_____

_____

_____

_____

_____

_____

_____

_____

_____

_____

_____

_____

_____

_____

_____

_____

_____

**Journal 3:**

_____

_____

_____

_____

_____

_____

_____

_____

_____

_____

_____

_____

_____

_____

_____

_____

_____

_____

_____

_____

# Journal 4:

**Journal 5:**

**Journal 6:**

_____

_____

_____

_____

_____

_____

_____

_____

_____

_____

_____

_____

_____

_____

_____

_____

_____

_____

_____

_____

**Journal 7:**

**Journal 8:**

**Journal 9:**

# DISCUSSION QUESTIONS

## Preface:

1. What does the term "hustle" mean to the men in the book? Does the term *hustle* mean the same to you and your friends?

2. Who are the men in your life that are teaching you *the art of the hustle*?

3. Using the **Preface,** define the term *hustle* in your own words.

4. What according to the **Preface**, prepared the men whose stories are in the to write their selections?

5. Why did they decide to write <u>The Art of the Hustle: Lessons in Becoming a Man</u>? In other words, what do they hope their audience will gain from reading it?

## The Hustling Begins at an Early Age, 1– 12

1. Why did the boy's father put him to work at the age of 12? Do you agree or disagree that this is anappropriate age for a boy to start working outside the home? Explain.

2. What factors in the boy's father's life developed his father's strong work ethic?

3. According to the author, what factors led him to becoming a mentor?

    _____

    _____

4. Through their mentoring, the men decided to keep some lessons about being a man that their fathers and others had taught them about being a man and to get rid of some lessons. Do you agree or disagree with their choices?

    _____

    _____

5. Why was David Moore so proud of his father? Do you think a young man today would be as proud of a father who did manual labor? Explain.

    _____

    _____

## The Village, 15-27

1. Why do you think the author started this narrative with the men in his community going hunting? Why do you think this event had such a powerful impact on his memory?

    _____

    _____

2. According to Elder Wall, what makes a man a *real father*? Do you think his definition of a *real father* should be applied to fathers today? Explain why or why not.

    _____

    _____

3. What was so special about the way his community "did Church"? Is it possible for communities to "do church" the same way today. Why or why not?

    _____

    _____

4. The author talks about how all the children in a community belong to all the adults in the community and how a neighbor lady gave him and a friend a whipping. Would this concept of shared parenting work in your community? Explain.

    _____

    _____

5.  In what ways did growing up as a member of multiple families help shape the author's definition of family?

    _____

    _____

6.  Why do you think the author says that just because there was drinking and a little bit of action on the weekend didn't make his neighborhood a bad place to live? Considering the entire selection, would you consider the neighborhood where he lived a good place to grow up? Explain.

    _____

    _____

    _____

7.  Why did the men at the YMCA make boys who wanted to fight settle their disagreements boxingone on one? How are arguments in your neighborhood usually settled? Which way is better? Explain.

    _____

    _____

8.  In your own words, describe the  kind of  Village  concept that might work in your community.

    _____

    _____

9.  What lesson or lessons about developing into manhood do you think this selection teaches?

    _____

    _____

## It's About the Family, p.p. 28-37

1. Throughout the selection, the author uses the terms grandparents, grandma, Dad, and mother to describe the relatives who raised him. Why do you think he does not distinguish among terms that usually have very different meanings?

   _____

   _____

2. Growing up, what were some of the most important things in the author's life and how did these things impact his life beyond his childhood?

   _____

   _____

3. The author describes a Swim Culture that includes dozens of large teams of excellent African American swimmers. Now, the majority of African American males are either non-swimmers andor average swimmers at best. Talk to your parents and grandparents about the reason or reasons they think Black Competitive Swim Teams disappeared.

   _____

   _____

4. The author relates a story about why his grandmother's recipes were lost when she died. Who inyour family is the best cook? What are you or others in your family doing to preserve those recipes?

   _____

   _____

5. What does the excerpt about Miss Lucy say about the kind of woman the author's mother was?

   _____

   _____

6. In your own words, relate the reason why the author believes that more marriages stayed together years ago. Do you think these ideas are applicable in today's culture?

   _____

   _____

7. What lesson or lessons about developing into manhood do you think this selection teaches?

_____

_____

8. What tradition from his childhood did the author continue after he was married. Why do you think he continued this tradition?

_____

_____

_____

# Unconditional Love, p.p. 39-45

1. Do you think there is a difference between getting a whipping and what A.J.'s father did to him? Explain.

_____

_____

2. What is A.J.'s definition of a good father? Would those same characteristics define a man as agood father today?

_____

_____

3. Do you agree with A.J. that the neighbors were unaware of what was happening to him? Explain.

_____

_____

4. A. J. excuses his mother's failure to intervene on his behalf. Do you feel that his excuses for hismother are acceptable reasons for her doing nothing?

_____

_____

5. What do you think your mother would have done under similar circumstances?

_____

_____

6. Since A.J.s Grandmother only lived a few blocks away, why do you think he had not gone

to her earlier?

_____

_____

7. If your father had treated you as A.J.'s father treated him, do think that you would
   have taken care of your father like A.J. did? Explain.

_____

_____

_____

8. The title of the selection is "Unconditional Love: A lesson in forgiveness." What does it
   mean to love a parent unconditionally?

_____

_____

9. What is the lesson in forgiveness that the author wants the reader to learn?

_____

_____

## When I was Nothing but a Boy, p.p. 46-53

1. The story of the dark forest describes the young boys as "feeling mannish." What does
   "feeling mannish" mean? What characteristics are attributed to being or acting mannish
   today?

_____

_____

2. Do you think fear is an effective method of making children behave? Explain.

_____

_____

3. Think of your friends, which one of them would be most likely to be the one to go into
   the dark forest? Why do you think he would be the one?

_____

_____

4. Do you agree or disagree that at some point a boy is too old to be disciplined by a parent? Explain.

_____

_____

5. In similar circumstances as Jam Man, what would you do?

_____

6. Do you think that your parent (s) discipline your sister (s) differently than they do you? Do you think that boys and girls need different forms of discipline? What form of discipline worked bestwith you?

_____

_____

_____

7. Do you remember a story from your childhood that taught you an important lesson?

_____

_____

## GUIDED LISTENING ACTIVITY

Before viewing the Video- **U Will Know-** Read the following questions before you listen to the song:

1. How did the boy view his future when he was young?

_____

_____

2. What changed the boy's view of his future as he grew older?

_____

_____

3. What did he do to make things better for himself?

_____

4. What is the first thing you must do to make the transition from boy to man?

_____

_____

5. What must you do when times get hard? What does the song tell you to do when life is so hard that it brings you to tears?

_____

_____

_____

6. In your own words, explain the meaning of the following line from the song.

   Just grab the <u>winds</u> and make demands

   And the vibe will take you far.

_____

_____

7. As you grow older, what will you know about life that you do not know now?

_____

_____

SONG NOTES: *Black Men United (B.M.U.) was a collaboration of many African American male R&B, neo soul and soul music artists. Its sole song "U Will Know", written by a young D'Angelo, was released in 1994. It was featured in the movie Jason's Lyric and on the movie's soundtrack. This group included Tevin Campbell, El DeBarge, Gerald LeVert, Tony Toni Toné, Boyz II Men, Al B. Sure, Lenny Kravitz, R. Kelly, Aaron Hall, Brian McKnight, Silk, Keith Sweat, Stokley, H-Town, and Christophe.*

**Point and click <u>ctrl</u> to follow the link.**

<u>Black Men United ~ U Will Know - YouTube</u>          (Skip any ads)

## U Will Know

Mmm...hmm...hmm...mmm...hmm...

Yeah, yeah


When I was a young boy

I had visions of fame

They were wild and they were free

And They were blessed with my name


And then I grew older

And I saw what's to see

That the world is full of pain

And my dreams they left me


And then I got stronger

Inside of the pain

That's when I picked up the pieces

And I regained my name


And I fought hard, y'all

To carve out  my place

And right now things ain't heavy

And it don't seem in vain


[Your dreams ain't easy] Your dreams ain't easy

[You just stick by your plan] You just stick by your plan

[Go from boys to men] Go from boys to men

[You must act like a man] You gotta act like a man

[When it gets hard, y'all] When it gets hard, y'all

[You just grab what you know] Got what you know

[Stand up tall and don't you fall] And my background sing

You will know [You will know], yeah...eah...

[You will know]

[You will know] You will know, you will know

[You will know]


And I know you're cryin'

'Cause it's all seems in vein

And the things you want you can't have

It just all went away


But life ain't over

Hoo...hoo...

Just grab the winds and make demands

And the vibe will take you far


[Your dreams ain't easy] Your dreams ain't easy

[You just stick by your plan] Stick by your plan, boy

[Go from boys to men] Go from boys to men

[You must act like a man] I know it ain't easy

[When it gets hard, y'all] it gets hard sometime

[You just grab what you know] Yes, it does

[Stand up tall and don't you fall] Stand up tall, don't you fall, and you will know, yeah

[You will know]

[You will know] Ah...ah...ah... (You will know)

[You will know] Hey, there's no doubt about it

[You will know] Hey, you will know


[You will know] You will know

[You will know] Hey...ey...hey...

[You will know] You will know, yeah

[Oh, you will know] Hey...


[Your dreams ain't easy] Your dreams ain't easy

[You just stick by your plan] Stick by your plans

[Go from boys to men] Boys to men

[You must act like a man] You must act like a man

[When it gets hard, y'all] It ain't hard, yeah

[You just grab what you know] Grab what you know

[Stand up tall and don't you fall] Oh...oh...oh...


[Your dreams ain't easy]

[You just stick by your plan] Hey...hey...yeah

[Go from boys to men] Boys to men

[You must act like a man] I know it ain't easy

[When it gets hard, y'all]

[You just grab what you know] Yeah...

[Stand up tall and don't you fall] Come on D and sing this song

[You will know] Yeah...

[You will know] You will know

[You will know]

[You will know] Hey...


[You will know]

[You will know]

[You will know]

[Oh, you will know]

8. As a team or small group write your version of this song including the lessons about life that you have learned. Also, include the things that have made your lives hard and what eases the pain or hard times in your life. Perform at the next major gathering.

_____

_____

_____

_____

_____

_____

_____

_____

_____

_____

_____

_____

_____

# What About Race, p.p. 54-69

1.  The author says that he did not understand the impact of being a person of a different race until he was twelve or thirteen. Do you think it is possible for a black boy to reach that age today with-out an understanding of this concept? Why?

    _____

    _____

2.  Why do you think two of the White Troops moved to the side of the camp where only Black Boy Scouts had lived for most of the summer?

    _____

    _____

3.  Ask your grandparents or other older adults about the race relations in your city or town duringthe fifties and sixties. Based on their responses, explain why it was so important for Black athletes to always beat all predominately White teams?

    _____

    _____

4.  At the end of the summer, how did the author feel about race relations?

    _____

    _____

5.  Why did he feel that the racial situation in the Boy Scouts was less stressful than the racial treatment in the military?

    _____

    _____

6.  What reason did the author give for racial problems in the military remaining unresolved? Do youthink this was the real reason?

    _____

    _____

    _____

7. What two factors made race relations better when the author was stationed in Texas?

_____

_____

8. Why do you think the military makes it an offense to make friends with native populations in foreign countries?

_____

_____

9. What working and living conditions led to the author's panic attack?

_____

_____

10. How did the author manage to get home from Turkey without official leave?

_____

_____

11. Do you think that the author's earlier experiences in the Boy Scouts and on the football team con-tributed to the problems he had in the military? Explain.

_____

_____

_____

12. What lesson (s) about racial relationships from this selection apply to racial relationships where you live?

_____

_____

_____

_____

_____

# My Brother's Keeper: Beyond Turning the Other Cheek, 70-78

1. Why do you think the young man was allowed to openly sell drugs on a busy street?

   _____

   _____

2. Why was the community so complacent about the young man selling drugs so close to a church?

   _____

   _____

3. Why do you think the author decided to "just talk" to the young man rather than calling the police?

   _____

   _____

4. What lesson did the author hope the young man would learn from his stories about his difficultchildhood?

   _____

   _____

5. Why didn't the author's story about his childhood get the results that he expected?

   _____

   _____

6. According to the young man, what is worse than having your father die? Do you agree with theauthor or the young man? Explain.

   _____

   _____

7. Do you agree or disagree that someone can learn some of the same lessons on the Street that canbe learned in the military? Explain.

   _____

   _____

8. Why do you think the concept of "that God thing" was so difficult for the young man to under-stand? How would you explain "that God thing" to him?

_____

_____

9. Why do you think the young man joined the church after the author left for another church?

_____

_____

## The Keys to Living Well, p.p. 52-57

1. What does the phrase "a man should be able to pull himself up by the bootstraps" mean to you? Do you agree or disagree with this theory? Explain.

_____

_____

2. The author makes a clear distinction between a stepfather and a Dad. Why do you think he does this?

_____

_____

3. What factors led to his selection of North Carolina A&T State University? Do you feel these factors are important when selecting a college to attend? Explain.

_____

_____

_____

4. Work with an older adult to make a chart to compare and contrast school today and school during the fifties, sixties, seventies, or eighties. Include factors like teachers, teacher expectations, methods of disciplining students, student interactions, grading, etc. Discuss your chart with thegroup.

| Past (1950s, 1960s, 1970s, 1980s) *Circle Years* | Present |
|---|---|
|  |  |
|  |  |
|  |  |
|  |  |
|  |  |

5. Are there ways that you could begin to prepare to live well in the future even though you are still young?

_____

_____

_____

6. Why do you think the author's mother did not just ask him for the $15.00?

_____

_____

7. What are the authors "keys" to living well? Which, if any, of these "keys" do you apply to your life?

_____

_____

_____

_____

# The King and Queen of the House, p.p. 86-92

1. How does the clear understanding of both the father's and mother's "place" or responsibilities in the family impact family living? Is there a clear understanding of the "place" or responsibilities of the members of your family?

_____

_____

2. In an earlier selection, the author described his mother as being _nurturing_. In your own words define the term _nurturing_.

_____

_____

3. List three of the factors that made the Warnersville Community a nurturing Community. Is the community where you live a _nurturing community_? Explain why the community where you live is or is not nurturing.

_____

_____

_____

_____

4. According to the author, what are some of the positive factors about growing up in a family of eleven children? What size is your family? List at least three positive factors in growing up ina family the size of yours.

_____

_____

_____

5. Select one of the three sayings that the author's father often repeated (p.88) and put it in your own words. If you had to rank the sayings as they apply to your life which one, would you say is the most important? Explain.

_____

_____

_____

6. Do you agree or disagree that watching how his father treated his mother is the most effective way for a father to teach his sons how to treat women. What has your father or the men aroundyour mother taught you about how to treat women?

_____

_____

_____

7. What impact do you think growing up in a home where there was no such thing as women's workor man's work had on the author's attitude towards women?

_____

_____

_____

8. Do you agree or disagree that fathers treating their sons affectionately makes the sons "soft"?
Explain.

_____

_____

_____

_____

_____

_____

_____

9.  **"Keep Ya Head Up"** is a song by Tupac Shakur. It addresses issues concerning lack of respect toward the female gender, especially poor black women. It has a very positive message andis often used as an example of Shakur's softer side.

https://www.youtube.com/watch?v=XW--
            IGAfeas

Many consider it to be one of the deepest rap songs ever made and it is often referenced by other artists in their work, building Shakur's persona as a very socially conscious and influential rapper. The song was voted #11 in About.com's Top 100 Rap Songs, with "Dear Mama" voted #4.

**DIRECTIONS: As you listen to the song, Highlight sections of the song that appear to be the answer(s) to the pre-listening questions or that will help you complete your list. Try to catalog (list) the reasons why women deserve respect and the ways in which some men disrespect women.**

### _Cataloging the reasons why women deserve respect:_

1.  _____

2.  _____

3.  _____

4.  _____

5.  _____

6.  _____

7.  _____

8.  _____

*Cataloging ways women are disrespected:*

1. _____

2. _____

3. _____

4. _____

5. _____

6. _____

7. _____

## "Keep Ya Head Up"

Little something for my godson Elijah
And a little girl named Corin

Some say the blacker the berry, the sweeter the juice
I say the darker the flesh then the deeper the roots
I give a holla to my sisters on welfare
2Pac cares if don't nobody else care
And I know they like to beat you down a lot
When you come around the block, brothers clown a lot
But please don't cry, dry your eyes, never let up
Forgive, but don't forget, girl, keep your head up
And when he tells you you ain't nothing, don't believe him
And if he can't learn to love you, you should leave him
'Cause, sister, you don't need him
And I ain't trying to gas ya up, I just call 'em how I see 'em
You know what makes me unhappy? When brothers make babies and leave a young mother to be a pappy
And since we all came from a woman
Got our name from a woman and our game from a woman
I wonder why we take from our women
Why we rape our women, do we hate our women?

I think it's time to kill for our women
Time to heal our women, be real to our women
And if we don't we'll have a race of babies
That will hate the ladies that make the babies
And since a man can't make one
He has no right to tell a woman when and where to create one
So will the real men get up?
I know you're fed up, ladies, but keep your head up

**Chorus**
Keep ya head up, ooh, child
Things are gonna get easier
Keep ya head up, ooh, child
Things'll get brighter
Keep ya head up, ooh, child
Things are gonna get easier
Keep ya head up, ooh, child
Things'll get brighter

Ayo, I remember Marvin Gaye used to sing to me
He had me feeling like black was the thing to be
And suddenly the ghetto didn't seem so tough
And though we had it rough, we always had enough
I huffed and puffed about my curfew and broke the rules
Ran with the local crew and had a smoke or two
And I realize momma really paid the price
She nearly gave her life to raise me right
And all I had to give her was my pipe dream
Of how I'd rock the mic and make it to the bright screen
I'm trying to make a dollar out of fifteen cents
It's hard to be legit and still pay the rent
And in the end it seems I'm heading for the pen
I try to find my friends, but they're blowing in the wind
Last night my buddy lost his whole family
It's gonna take the man in me to conquer this insanity
It seems the rain'll never let up
I try to keep my head up and still keep from getting wet up
You know, it's funny, when it rains it pours
They got money for wars but can't feed the poor
Say there ain't no hope for the youth
And the truth is it ain't no hope for the future
And then they wonder why we crazy
I blame my mother for turning my brother into a crack baby
We ain't meant to survive, 'cause it's a set-up
And even though you're fed up

Huh, you got to keep your head up

**Chorus**
Keep ya head up, ooh, child
Things are gonna get easier
Keep ya head up, ooh, child
Things'll get brighter
Keep ya head up, ooh, child
Things are gonna get easier
Keep ya head up, ooh, child
Things'll get brighter

And uh, to all the ladies having babies on they own
I know it's kinda rough and you're feeling all alone
Daddy's long gone and he left you by your lonesome
Thank the Lord for my kids even if nobody else want 'em
'Cause I think we can make it, in fact, I'm sure
And if you fall, stand tall and comeback for more
'Cause ain't nothing worse than when your son
Wants to know why his daddy don't love him no mo'
You can't complain you was dealt this
Hell of a hand without a man, feeling helpless
Because there's too many things for you to deal with
Dying inside, but outside you're looking fearless
While tears is rolling down your cheeks
You steady hoping things don't fall down this week
'Cause if it did, you couldn't take it
And don't blame me, I was given this world, I didn't make it
And now my son's getting older and older and colder
From having the world on his shoulders
While the rich kids is driving Benz
I'm still trying to hold on to surviving friends
And it's crazy, it seems it'll never let up
But please, you got to keep your head up

**Directions:** Discuss your lists with your group. What would you add to either list?

What does Tupac say will happen to  boys who grow up hating and disrespecting the ladies?

_____

_____

## Mastering Time Management, p.p. 93-99

1.  What impact did the death of his 24-year-old father have on the author's family?

    _____

    _____

2.  Why do you think it took his grandfather a year to take custody of his grandsons? What circum-stances might lead to the court granting full custody  or guardianship to a grandparent?

    _____

    _____

3.  Why do you think the author honors and respects his grandfather so deeply? Is there someone inyour life to whom you would give the same level of respect and honor?

    _____

    _____

4.  What three factors does the author blame for nearly failing his freshman year in college?

    _____

    _____

5.  One of the authors professors gives him some advice for managing his time. What methods oftime management would you add to the professor's advice?

    _____

    _____

6.  Do you feel that the authors rational for remaining in ROTC even though he was failing most ofhis classes was a sound reason?

    _____

    _____

7.  Make a list of at least three reasons why you feel that you would be successful in college if youdecide to go. List any factors that may impede your success.

    _____

    _____

    _____

8. At the end of the selection, the author pays homage to some of the people whom he says helpedto make him the man he is today. Who are some of the people to whom you would pay homagefor where you are now in your life?

_____

_____

_____

## Lessons Well Learned, p.p.100-104

1. What reasons does the author give for money being tight when he was growing up?

_____

_____

2. The author says, "Like most children of divorced parents, I was not completely sure of the rea-sons for the divorce." How much of the reasons for the parents' divorce should be shared with the children? If information is shared, how should it be done?

_____

_____

3. According to the author, how did his mother's lack of stable relationships impact his childhood?

_____

_____

4. In your opinion, was Lee a good adult male role model for a teenage young man? Explain.

_____

_____

5. What is more important wining a fight or the way you win it? Explain your choice.

_____

_____

6. What 'well learned lesson (s) did this selection teach?

_____

_____

7. What are some ways that you can tell someone off without using cuss words?

_____

_____

## Be Ready! Be Ready!  p.p.105-112

1. In what ways was  this author's childhood different from many other men of his generation?

_____

_____

2. What, according to the  author, was a worst punishment than getting a whipping? What is the worst form of punishment that you receive?

_____

_____

3. Why was going to church an important mainstay of the author's life? What are the important mainstays in your life?

_____

_____

4. Reword the authors father's favorite quotes in today's vernacular (the way young people of yourgeneration talk).

_____

_____

5. How did the author prepare as a child and as a young man to be ready when opportunities to excel were presented to him?

_____

_____

6. What did the author do when he was given petty jobs that no one else wanted to do? How did this help him in the future? Explain.

_____

_____

_____

7.  Choose one word that you feel best describes this author and explain your choice.

_____

_____


## Mighty Men Move Others to Greatness, p.p. 113-120

1.  Why do you think the author began his selection with Golden Frinks instead of one of the morefamous Civil Rights leaders that he met?

_____

_____

2.  Summarize the lessons about life that the author learned from his experiences as Frinks' driver? Have you spent any time interacting with a man who you feel will have a similar impact on yourlife? Briefly talk about him and how he has possibly "moved" you to greatness one day.

_____

_____

3.  Why did having Dr. Benjamin Mays speak at his graduation have such an impact on the author?

_____

_____

4.  With which of the Civil Rights leaders that are mentioned in the selection other than Dr. MartinLuther King were you already familiar? Do additional research on one of the ones that you knew little or nothing about and share it at your next meeting.

_____

_____

5.  The author became upset with his parents when he discovered that other boys his age were  receiving allowances. Have you ever been upset with your parent (s) over something one of your peers had or was allowed to do? Explain.

_____

_____

6. Debate with one team representing the father and the other team the author: **Resolve** that every young man of a certain age deserves an allowance for chores performed in and around his home.

# The Debate Worksheet
**The debate will consist of four rounds.**

**PROPOSITION:** Resolve that every young man of a certain age deserves an allowance for chores performed in and around his home.

## Round 1
Opening Statement – proposition then opposition (Circle PROPOSITION or OPPOSITION)
The Captain defines the Motion and briefly summarizes why their team is arguing for or against the Motion. (1 team member) Discuss your position with your team and write a brief statement as to why your position is right.

_____

_____

_____

## Round 2
Main Arguments – PROPOSITION then OPPOSITION

Team members present their main arguments either for or against the Motion. (2 to 4 team members). List your groups three strongest arguments and place any information that you fine to support those arguments on note cards.
Argument 1: _____

_____

Argument 2: _____

_____

Argument_____

_____

## Round 3: Cross-Examination – opposition asks proposition questions first
The teams now have a chance to question each other. (3 to 8 team members)
In your group, think about the questions that the other side might ask and come up with plausible answers to those questions. For example, one argument for boys of a certain age getting money for the work that they do around the house might be that boys of a certain have personal expenses. If you are the Proposition you may want to think of what these expenses might be.

**Questions** (Opposition)

_____

_____

_____

_____

_____

**Answers** (Proposition)

_____

_____

_____

_____

_____

**Round 4: Closing Statement** – opposition then proposition

The teams sum up their arguments, what they have achieved in the debate and they appeal to the Floor (Judges), explaining why they should vote for their side of the argument. (2 to 3 team members).
Closing Statement:

_____

_____

_____

7.  At this point in your life, what are some of the lessons that you have learned that you think you will take with you for the rest of your life?

_____

_____

_____

# Family, God, and Country, p.p. 121-128

1.  Of all the things that have happened to you during your lifetime, which ones do you think were of your own making or were your fault? Explain.

_____

_____

2.  Have you ever had an experience that made you feel the way the author describes in the firstparagraph? If you have, describe that experience.

_____

_____

3.  What do you think motivated the author to disobey his father's "house rules"?

_____

_____

4. What are the "house rules" in your home? Do you feel that those rules are too strict? Explain.

_____

_____

5. If you went home and found your clothes packed up on the front porch, what would you do?

_____

_____

6. Do you have siblings? If so, do you have a special relationship with one of them? If you do not have siblings, do you have a parent or other relative with whom you are particularly close? Whydo you think you are particularly close with this person?

_____

_____

_____

7. Why does the home-place that he left as a young adult mean so much to the author now? Do youhave a home-place that induces similar feelings for you? Explain.

_____

_____

8. People say, "That time heals all wounds." In your experience, do wounds like the death of a close relative heal over as time passes?

_____

_____

## Creating Leaders, p.p. 129-144

1. List at least three reasons why the author is proud of his mother's side of the family, the Millers.List at least three reasons why you are proud of your mother's family.

_____

_____

2. What aspects of the Miller side of his family does the author imply that he is less proud of? Are there aspects of either side of your family that you feel the same way about?

_____

_____

3. Do you think that the author's father, Ernest, thought through his actions on the day his team won the baseball game? Give reasons for your answer.

_____

_____

4. List three reasons why the author was proud of his father and his father's side of the family.

_____

_____

5. What factors differentiated the two sides of the author's family? Do those factors still matter today?

_____

_____

6. Why do you think the promises that the author's father demanded of him were so important to his father?

_____

_____

7. In what ways did attending an historically Black college help the author get in touch with his culture? With the coming of integration and more racially mixed neighborhoods, do you think connecting with one's culture is still important? Explain.

_____

_____

_____

8. Select one of the myths about leadership and expand on the author's brief explanation as to why the myth is false. Use examples from your own experiences or the experiences of others close to you in your explanation.

_____

_____

_____

_____

_____

_____

_____

_____

_____

_____

_____

_____

## I Still Laugh when I Think About It, p.p. 145-148

1. In two-three paragraphs relate a story from your youth that makes you smile or laugh yearslater. Share your story with the group.

_____

_____

_____

_____

_____

_____

_____

_____

**THE END**

# Leaving a Legacy, p.p. 149-155

1. What do you think were the advantages of having three strong women involved the author's upbringing? Can you think of any possible disadvantages?

   _____

   _____

   _____

2. What can fathers do to leave their sons a legacy of integrity or character?

   _____

   _____

   _____

3. Do you agree or disagree that the way a father lives before his son is more important than what hetells his son? Explain.

   _____

   _____

   _____

4. When do you think, a man should begin to build his legacies? Explain why you feel that age is appropriate.

   _____

   _____

5. According to the author, the most difficult legacy to leave is a financial legacy. Do you think thisstatement will be true for you? Explain.

   _____

   _____

6. What kind of spiritual legacy do you plan to leave behind? What are you doing now to build thatlegacy?

7. Do you agree or disagree that going to prison does not necessarily damage one's legacy of character? Explain.

_____

_____

8. Do you think that it is possible for parents and their children to "make up" for loss time whenthey have been separated for a long period of time? Explain what you think should be done tohelp bridge the gap.

_____

_____

_____

9. What particular piece of advice from the selection about building a financial legacy do you "see"yourself using now?

_____

_____

## Summary Activity

1.  In one or two paragraphs, briefly explain the lessons found in the book and how they could orcould not be applied to your life. Discuss what you have written with your group. Did anyonetalk about getting something different out of the selections in the book than you did?

_____

_____

_____

_____

_____

_____

_____

_____

_____

_____

_____

_____

_____

_____

_____

_____

_____

# The Art of the Hustle Vocabulary

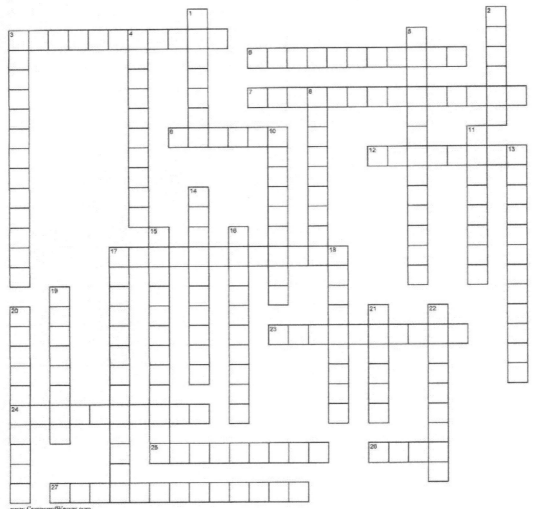

www.CrosswordWeaver.com

## ACROSS

3 somebody who initiates a legal prosecution
6 confidence in your own merit as an individual person
7 somebody whose job is to manage the affairs of a business, organization, or institution
9 somebody, usually older and more experienced , who advises and guides a younger, less experienced person
12 a person who encourages somebody or something to grow, develop, thrive, and to be successful
17 the relation between the result and its cause
23 to empty the mind of thoughts, or concentrate the mind on one thing, in order to aid mental or spiritual development, comtemplation, or relaxation
24 a feeling of enthusiasm, interest, or commitment that makes somebody want to do something, or something that causes such a feeling
25 honest and open in relationships with others
26 an agreement made between two or more people of groups, either formally or informally, to do something together or for each other
27 to bring legal charges against someone

## DOWN

1 an assurance that something will be done or will not be done
2 a city in New Jersey that is the preimary setting of the book The Pact

3 to have greater importance, power, or influence than others
4 the end, as the culmination of a process; most importantly, when all things are considered
5 social pressure on somebody to adopt a type of hevaior, dress, or attitude in order to be accepted as part of a group
8 something that encourages or motivates somebody to do something
10 a period of supervised medical pratice after completing medical school
11 a low income housing development, usually with multiple families living in several buildings
13 to help somebody to return to good health or a normal life by providing training or therapy
14 the mutual feeling of trust and affection and the behavior that typify relationships between friends
15 daunting; instilling fear, awe, or a sense of inadequacy
16 the subjects taught at an educational institution, or the topics within a subject
17 a condition that affects what happens or how somebody reacts in a particular situation
18 an environment that is able to resist disturbance caused by environmental changes, or the ability to return to its original state after disturbance
19 a group of people or things that is a small part of a much larger group
20 a worthy person who is a good example for other people
21 somebody who comes from a country of Latin America
22 the quality of possessing and steadfastly adhering to high moral principles or professional standards

60

## Puzzle Word List:

administrators, circumstances, consequences. curriculum, friendship, genuinely, incentive, integrity, intimidating, Latino, meditating, mentor, minority, motivation, Newark, nurturer, pact, peer-pressure, predominately, press-charges, projects, promise, prosecutors, rehabilitate, residency, role-model, self-esteem, stability, ultimately

# Paideia Seminar: The Art of the Hustle
## *Suggested Post Reading Activities*

## Pre-activities

- The mentees will review the goals for Seminar.
- The mentees will review the Paideia Seminar rubric (see Index).
- Mentees will set a personal goal for the Seminar.
- Mentor will state the objectives for reading the book
  Mentee will read the book, *The Art of the Hustle: Lessons in Becoming A Man*

## Activities

### Seminar

1. Once the students have read the book , the mentor shall pose an opening question to begin the Seminar: "Of the themes that we discussed in the Pre-Reading Activity, which one do you think the authors would agree was the single most important lesson for readers to learn? What leads youto believe that?"

2. Once the discussion gets going, the mentor can ask prompting questions to guide the discussion in the proper direction. These questions will also check the students' comprehension of the text.

> *It was the life-long closeness that I felt for my brothers and sister on that side of the family rather than the fact that he was my biological father that influenced me to help them with him during his last days. That family closeness came from the way we did family and theway we did church as an extended family when I was growing up.*

> *The village was just there for all of us. We were connected to the village from day one.Back then, neighborhoods throughout the South were segregated. Whether it was in the Bot- toms in Kentucky, the Eastside in Dunn, North Carolina, the Eastside in High Point, or the*
> *Nocho Park Community in Greensboro some things were very much the same- home was there;family was there; school was there; and all the people who cared about us were there.*

Most of narrators site the "village," church, and family as huge influences on their lives. Discuss how one of the narrators was affected by one or more of these factors.

How did family relationships influence the lives of the men? What stands out toyou about each of their childhood experiences at home?

Each of the narrators describes a turning point at which specific decisions or choices—to become a personal driver for a civil rights leader, to leave the military, to become a mentor, to leave home, to study harder—changed thecourse of their lives. Are such moments recognizable only in hindsight? Doyou think that shaping the events of your life into a story would influence the importance you placed on specific events?

3. Before the discussion ends, the mentor should ask the following closing questions:
   - What are the consequences for allowing "family expectations" or peer pressure to influence yourdecisions?
   - How does it affect the lives of the characters in the book?
   - How have "family expectations" or friends who are being brought up differently from you affect-ed your life?

## Research project

1. The mentees will select a person who has changed the lives of others. They will conduct on-line research and write an essay which will discuss what the individual had to overcome to be successful and how this person has impacted the lives of others. The essay should focus on one or more of the themes of the book, *The Art of the Hustle* (Family, church, education, service to others, role models,consequences, etc.) and link to the theme of their own lives.

2. Students will use the information in their essay to produce a presentation that incorporates technology and writing skills, in order to inform the group about the individual they researched.

## Assessment

Mentees will complete a self-evaluation by using the Personal Seminar Rating Chart (see Appendix for Personal Seminar Rating Chart)

# Appendix
Common Debate Rules, p. 68-69
Personal Seminar Rating Chart, p.70

# COMMON DEBATE RULES FOR CLASSROOMS

## Common Courtesy During Debate

Debates often focus on controversial topics that students may feel passionately about, so courtesy and respect for all opinions should be encouraged. To introduce the idea of courtesy, explain to students that debate questions often do not have a "right" or "wrong" answer and that critical thinking develops when different ideas are present. For example, set ground rules for interrupting, raised voices and personal attacks before starting the debate. The High School Public Debate Program allows heckling limited to a single word or phrase directed at the judges. However, interruptions or exclamations that disrupt the speaker or are excessively rude are not allowed. The penalty for breaking rules in competitive debate include taking a loss, having to repeat the debate or a reprimand.

## 2 Rules for Topics

Rules for choosing topics attempt to ensure that both the pro and con sides of the subject can be researched. In classroom debates, teachers provide the topics, often based on the class subject. For example, in an English class, students may debate whether fate actually guides the human experience after reading *Oedipus Rex*. In a history class, students may debate the merits of war, while a science class may debate the ethics of bioengineering. When choosing topics for the classroom, teachers should consider the political climate of the school as well as the maturity and sensitivity of the students involved. Teachers should also avoid topics that reveal personal bias or may easily lead to attacks on individual students.

## 3 Argument and Proof

With an assigned topic, both the pro and con sides in the debate should begin to research evidence for their side of the argument. Debaters should use both facts and opinions in the presentation of their argument. Students should also research the opposing side and perform a critical analysis to decide which facts and opinions of the other side will be used in the rebuttal stage. In competitive debate, the use of electronics during debate is not allowed, but classroom debates may allow this. Evidence should be in the form of facts, not other speeches, or opinions, and the first mention of evidence should include a complete citation -- author, title, date of publication and page number.

## 4 Rules for Speakers

To ensure that all opinions are heard, develop a format for engaging in debate and introduce the format to the students before the debate. For example, the debate may include two rounds of discussion in which the first side presents the "pro" side immediately followed by the team with the "con" side. The second round will allow the "pro" side to respond to the "con" arguments of the first round. Create time limits for each side that are clear and carefully adhered to. For example, give each side a two-minute limit to present its case.

# Personal Seminar Rating Chart

Personal Goals:

Rate yourself 1 - 5, with 1 being your BEST and 5 being your WORST.  Be honest !

_____I came prepared for seminar.

_____I was courteous to the other group members.

_____I paused and thought before speaking.

_____I listened to others tell their ideas.

_____I kept an open mind for opinions different from my own.

_____I acted as a positive role model for other students.

_____I built on other ideas before I gave my own opinion.

_____I reflected on the text.

_____I felt comfortable speaking during seminar.

_____I spoke clearly.

_____I interrupted others.

_____I acted silly.

_____I did not look at the person speaking.

_____I spoke off topic.

_____I talked too much.

Made in the USA
Columbia, SC
07 August 2023

21223253R00039